Smoke from the Fires

Michael Dennis Browne

SMOKE
FROM THE
FIRES

Carnegie-Mellon University Press
Pittsburgh 1985

For Lisa

ACKNOWLEDGMENTS

Aspen Anthology, Atlantic Monthly, bits, Black Box, Epoch, FallOut, Greenfield Review, Ironwood, Kayak, Milkweed Chronicle, News of the Universe (Sierra Club Books), Northwest Review, The Poet Dreaming in the Artist's House (Milkweed Editions), Poetry on the Buses (Pittsburgh), Prairie Schooner, Research, Steelhead, Storystone, Studio One.

I am very grateful to the National Endowment for the Arts, the Graduate School of the University of Minnesota and the Bush Foundation for generous support which enabled me to take time to work on this book.

The publication of this book is supported by grants from the National Endowment for the Arts in Washington, D.C., a Federal agency, and by the Pennsylvania Council of the Arts.

CONTENTS

HIDE AND GO SEEK

for Lisa

I count to fifty.
Then I appear at the French window;
in my hand, the three-flame candelabrum.
The children have run to hide in my sister's garden.
It is March, damp dark, that English dark I left.

I make the monster sound.
I give the groan they long to hear, and fear.
I can almost feel their shivering out there.

Then I begin to move.
I lurch, stiff-legged. I sway.
I am the Mud Man, come
still smeared from his swamp,
I am something extinct
with my rotting fingers,
I am the slimy thing from the sea
who leaks after them on feet
horribly like the human hand, but heavier.
I am he no longer afraid of fire,
who points these prongs of flame to find them.
I need some blood.
I need to catch me some family flesh
and chew it down to the bone.

Appalled, they hurtle all over,
the nephews, the nieces,
they scatter, they stream
round Fran and Angela's garden,
desperate scared , mad scared —
who let this thing loose in England? —
run! run! —
the Bogey Man, the Bog Beast —
run! run!
Roaring, reaching out,

again and again I miss them,
so slow I am,
so sleepy with my swampy blood,
miss them just enough to freshen their fear,
to send them screaming further
into the dark,

out behind the beanpoles,
behind the compost,
behind the favorite tree that is now
metal to the touch.
I hear, I hear the panting.

And — it is enough. Now it is done.
Now I raise the candles to show
my friendlier face — I am Michael again,
the almost American uncle,
and I call to them: *All in, All in.*
Together we go toward the house,
through the garden that is theirs again,
laughing, still thrilled with our fright.
And Damien, my godson, four,
that boy of light I sought in the dark,
shouts: "I'm bigger than myself!"

Whoever the seekers, children,
whoever will chase you,
if inside you, if behind you,
may they miss, I pray it,
may they not touch,
may you make it
past such grasping and reach the house
as now together we do,
where people are waiting who love us
and from darkness welcome us.
O mystery of family. O darkness. O house.
I pray it: *All in. All in.*

LAMB

Saw a lamb being born.
Saw the shepherd chase and grab a big ewe
and dump her on her side.
Saw him rub some stuff from a bottle on his hands.
Saw him bend and reach in.
Heard two cries from the ewe.
Two sharp quick cries. Like high grunts.
Saw him pull out a slack white package.
Saw him lay it out on the ground.
Saw him kneel and take his teeth to the cord.
Saw him slap the package around.
Saw it not move.
Saw him bend and put his mouth to it and blow.
Doing this calmly, half kneeling.
Saw him slap it around some more.
Saw my mother watching this. Saw Angela. Saw Peter.
Saw Mimi, with a baby in her belly.
Saw them standing in a row
by the drystone wall, in the wind.
Saw the package move.
Saw it was stained with red and yellow.
Saw the shepherd wipe red hands on the ewe's wool.
Heard the other sheep in the meadow calling out.
Saw the package shaking its head.
Saw it try to stand. Saw it nearly succeed.
Saw it have to sit and think about it a bit.
Saw a new creature's first moments of thinking.
Felt the chill blowing through me.
Heard the shepherd say:
"Good day for lambing. Wind dries them out."
Saw the package start to stand. Get half-way. Kneeling.
Saw it push upward. Stagger, push, and make it.
Stand. Standing.
Saw it surely was a lamb, a lamb, a lamb!
Saw a lamb being born.

TO MY BROTHER PETER, ON THE BIRTH OF HIS FIRST CHILD

You who love to climb
the mountains you live among,
now you are roped to someone;
and when one day you fall,
as you will,
why, you've a son to swing from.

AT FORTY

1

There begin to be
shadows that only the leaves can make
there begin to be
mornings the body can open in

There begin to be
nests in the neighborhood
and one is across the street from me
in the low crotch of an elm

Already the ripe songs have started
before dawn   before dawn
and in darkness

2

My mother keeps calling from England.
She asks:
          "Are you happy?
          Are you happy?"

Yesterday I called *her*.
She said:
          "I've been sitting outside, darning.
          The weather's been glorious.
          My legs swelled up from the sun."

One morning last week she called,
as I overslept,
my mother waking me still
and this time just in time
to get me up
and to where I should be,

my mother from over an ocean
still getting her aging boy
out into the world . . .

3

I think my own songs are changing.
I think my mother would not know me
in some of the things I do.
She has passed on
her sentimentality to me,
though I can be colder too.

The blackbird's song reminds me of her.
But though there is only one mother,
and she wears out,
the blackbirds keep coming and coming,
packed with song;
and for each tree of my street
diseased and removed,
a young one replaces it.
But when my mother is taken,
only a space where she stood,
and these birds' singing
not be diminished one note.

If I could learn such detachment,
and not call it cruelty,
I could keep right on singing,
oblivious among leaves,
whatever family or friends
went down around me.

My mother,
the Buddha does not ask:
        "Are you happy?
        Are you happy?"
I dare not answer you,

except to say:
       "Oh yes. Oh no.
       You know."
I'd like to be cooler,
to sing clearer songs.

4

I start to feel
how old the light is,
that any dawn, however
ripe it seems, however recent,
has let too many go to hear
every clause of *my* claim on it,
that it asks me up
out of my pities, my pleading,
maybe to make a sterner,
maybe a less individual, song.

There begin to be
shadows that only the distant can cast
there begin to be
leaves that only the unseen let fall

Already the great songs have started
before dawn, Mother   in May
before dawn
and in darkness.

MRS MUM IN THE NEW WORLD

She sits in the apartment in town and stares out
at the street for hours, fascinated with the American
neighborhood, the exits, the entrances, all of a
midwestern morning. She sips cold white wine from my
christening cup.

Everyone I introduce her to, she kisses. She says:
"It's my form of salutation to the New World."

Her legs and ankles are very swollen. At the airport
she winced as she walked but she didn't talk about it and
kept on going, leaning on her cane.

When I cut my foot on a piece of glass and bleed
badly, she stoops, arthritic, and shows me how to press
on the wound so the blood congeals. "Press it," she
says, "like this, tight." She finds a roll of bandage
in her bag and winds it round my foot, fixes it with
a pin. I feel about ten. She says: "The ball of the
foot has the toughest skin."

Sitting up in bed one morning, fishing for money
in her bag. "Will ten dollars buy a bottle of milk?"
I say: "Gimme a twenty."

When we come to the north woods house, named for
the English one she bore me in, who but she would walk
up and kiss the wood of it? Who but Mrs Mum would thank
Eddie, my dear dead father, for her safe arrival there?

Me explaining to Nora Louise, her twin sister, not
to be scared in these woods at night. I say: "You can
hear the loons calling to each other in the dark." And
Nora Louise: "Are they *men*?"

She stands at the kitchen sink, washing her hair
with soap. She did it like this as a girl. "We had no
bathroom," she says, "and the toilet was out in the back."
She pours cup after cup over her head for rinsing.

Some leaves have yellowed already around the
screenhouse. And bugs draw bright blood from my mother.

In a lawn chair by the lake, at the swimming spot,
where we splash and shampoo and clown around, she'll
recite a childhood poem if we bully her, the one about
the little worm out in the rain, or, in her clear
girl's voice, something of Puck's, or a fairy song,
or, from that isle of sounds and sweet airs:

> *Where the bee sucks, there suck I;*
> *In a cowslip's bell I lie;*
> *There I couch when owls do cry.*
> *On a bat's back I do fly*
> *After summer merrily.*

"I won't be back," says Mrs Mum. Who loves it here.
She sits for hours. She sits to watch and hear the aspens
rattling in the wind, the wind-chimes ringing. Sometimes
she's light as a bird. She says little. She sits with
wine. She hums the wedding march she walked to once.
She stares into the leaves.

2

DREAM AT THE DEATH OF JAMES WRIGHT

The wind is rolling the buffalo down;
the wind is shining and sharpening the buffalo
and rolling them down.
The sheep have already scattered
toward the forest,
sheep are streaming
along the stained edges of the forest.
But the wind is rolling the buffalo down.
We have not built a shelter for them,
we have put up no corral.
They don't know enough to
come together, bind their black fur
together, sit out the storm.
I see one huge one struggling
inside a lantern of grasses.
The wind is rolling the buffalo down,
shining and sharpening them
and rolling them down.

3/26/80

LITTLE WOMEN

These little women have gray hair.
They wear print frocks and ankle socks.
Their hair is cropped.
Two days from Christmas, a mild snow.
As one by one I meet them,
Ruth tells me their names.
One kisses my hand.
One will not look at me.
One shudders and weeps on a couch.
One sways like a prize fighter,
rocking backwards and forwards on fixed feet,
throwing small punches.
One grinds her jaw around.
One sits smiling, as if at a wedding.
It is snowing, it is snowing.
Someone is being married in the snow.

For these gray girls I sing.
"A little child on the earth has been born."
It is the Flemish Carol,
which my father taught me.
"He came to earth but no home did He find."
The bare hall echoes like a bathroom,
I sing full-throated,
I feel like a bird among branches.
Do they hear? Do they hear the child's story?
I don't know how unraveled they are
behind those eyes,
I don't know if the doors

are closed or burning or whirling.
They seem like Ophelias who survived the stream.
Someone is being married.

Ruth circles with some of them. Dancing.
They shuffle and stamp. It is snowing.
"He came to the earth for the sake of us all.
He came to the earth for the sake of us all."
When later I ask Ruth
who, of all the minds at the institution,
are the most lost, she tells me
it is these.

THINKING OF TREES, JANUARY

Trees I have never seen, trees
whose trunks I can touch, dreaming
of trees by the sea.

My visible life I think of
as foliage, the story is in the foliage,
but the roots go on down.

I dream of trees by the sea,
whose trunks I can touch.

Some nights I upend,
all that thick earth-head wriggling,
all my sea of dark roots running.

Then is my speech life
dipped a little into silence
and comes up altered at dawn.

Trees I dream of, trees
by the sea,
and the woman whose face
is among the leaves.
But the one I want is the other,
she who is sleeping
deep in the grain of the tree.

FUCHSIA

for Lois Shelton

Fuchsia,
when I was in Arizona,
in the desert museum,
and saw the sweet acacia
flowering in February,
effortlessly yellow.
the acacia stretching
"from Arizona to Argentina,"

I thought of you
in the northern window,
how you struggle,
how your small buds bulge,
how you heave out
pale blossoms with tendrils
that drop to the desk,
how you conjure others.

Fuchsia,
when I was in Arizona,
I thought of you,
I thought of my father,
I thought of the dead
who endlessly flower,
I thought of my mother,
whom I can still talk to.
Fuchsia,
when I was among the acacia
I dreamed of you, huge,
like a head of wild hair
flared in the winter window.

TORTOISE SHELL, MOJAVE DESERT

for Lamar and Jim

We are kneeling in the sand by the shell. "He
must have run out of gas," Jim says. Underneath the
death cap, slightly damper sand. Green is growing
there. Lamar says: "His own small lawn!" Soft as
cress or alfalfa sprouts.

A jet goes over, high. I hear, but don't look
up. The pilot must be watching his instrument panel.
He's too busy in his plane to be lonely.

This shell looks lonely. Jim thinks a coyote
might have got him. At water-holes, he says, a coyote
will drink side by side with a tortoise or jackrabbit,
and only later kill him.

I swig some red wine, I toast the tortoise. I have
photographed the shell and its little lawn also. I get
depressed, thinking this writing could be too glib. I
don't want to be the pilot, coolly checking the
instruments of the poem. I would rather be holding
the tortoise shell, handling it. How dry, how ancient
it feels.

Once I picked up a tortoise in the north woods. The
small beaky head scared me, swinging around from out
of the thick body. But when I turned him over, I gasped
at the underside — like a cathedral window of flesh!
It was as if several hundred dawns were stamped into
its skin.

Jim and Lamar have gone on. Before I leave, I pick
up the shell and put it on my head. I stand there for

a while, eyes closed. I want to feel what his dying
might have taught him. It is a little death, but
I can learn from it. I wear his remnant awhile.

The shell sits sharp on either temple. When I
have put it back down, I see red on my finger — it
must be from where the shell cut into my scalp. No,
it's only ink. I place the shell back over its lawn,
so the growing can go on.

WARRIOR WITH SHIELD

(Henry Moore, 1953)

1

As if he had crawled from the sea.

Like a son beaten down
by the dark father century
or by the mother of centuries mutilated

he sits.

He will not go back to that sea
though his bronze reminds me
of its weeds crushed inward.

It seems he could yet swivel,
that with the one good arm
and shield clipped onto muscle
he still could sweep an enemy away.
Whoever hacked him elsewhere
should step with care here.

Eyes holes. Mouth a small
star-burst, as when a meteor
hurts the earth.
Where halves of the face should meet,
where there should be seam —

fissure.

As if with our own hands

we might complete you.
As if you had crawled to us for completion.
As if you were ours to grow.

2

*No more
to wither in me. No more
to be made of me.*

*Nothing
for fathering, mothering. Done.
Caresses, none.*

*I have been hunted down
to my last shape.*

*But in you, near the echoing
heart a silence, bear me.
I am*

*the icon of the incomplete
in you. As I am, as I will
never be, live with me.*

CHINA, SEPTEMBER

I want to take
off layer after
layer
have been thinking
of the house in October
how I want to follow
the curve of the fall
down, dig my
wings down

and of China here,
now

I want to live in both worlds
I want to live in both worlds

Let a leaf I come upon
near the house
be China

let a frost
let a dew

Send a bird by
the window some time
across my line of sight
to remind me

Beijing

FIVE HUNDRED AND EIGHT BUDDHAS

for Jim White

In the Temple of the Azure Clouds, Jim,
there are five hundred and eight Buddhas.
I never saw so many Buddhas together before.
They're all made of wood,
all covered with gold-leaf,
all life-size.
They're seated on long raised platforms
and you look up into their faces
as you walk between them.

These Buddhas have the finest faces —
broad, powerful mouths and eyes —
and the tops of their heads are gold domes.
They all look terribly happy, terribly wise.

And this one has one knee lifted,
and this one has his two hands in the air
and he's grinning,
this one is holding a small fox-like animal,
and this one has a little head looking out
from where his heart is,
and this one's looking a bit cheeky,
and this one is holding scrolls,
and this one is tilting a jug;
Chang, my guide, bends and puts his mouth
under the jug a moment,
and I say: "He's pouring wisdom
and you need lots of it.
Badly in need of wisdom!"
And this one is carrying his wrinkled old mother
on his back,
and this one is sitting with his arm round his friend.

It is a Golden Parliament.
It is a Brotherhood.
It is a Hall of Buddhahood.
Professor Zheng beside me says:
"A childish simplicity, huh?"
These shame the statues of the Sacred Heart
and all the plaster saints I was raised on.

And they are all smiling.
These are the happiest people
I've seen in China so far.
And they're much happier than all the poets.
What happens to us?

And he with both hands held out,
and he with his palms spread,
he seems thrilled with some secret,
and he with his right leg
flat across under his left knee,
and his mouth open, wide open,
and he with a kind of cap,
almost Mickey Mouse, Disneyland almost,
and this very fierce one,
with a mouth slightly twisted,
with a radiant tail behind him
like a peacock fan,
he has a kind of . . . Shiva . . .
there's a Shiva-like quality to that one . . .
The Dancer, Jim, the Great Dancer.

And some are in
not such a good state of repair,
some need some help here and there,
people have scraped little bits of gold off them.
But there's nothing they can scrape
from the spirit, nor the heart,

not that.

I am among the Great Teachers.
I am in their garden.
And not only am I walking in that garden
but swimming slow
in the Buddha water,
slow among the sunken Buddha treasures,
my deep Brothers,
my deep Sisters,
little fish that I am,
I'm out of my shallows,
deep in the Buddha water,
and many I love and care for
are here in my breathing.

FOR THE CHINESE POET ZHENG MIN

1

I'm leaving. I'm giving you my pen —
a gift, not a grand one, a common pen,
with its ordinary ink. It leaks, even,
you'll find that out.
But a pen, a green one.
You who have done my poems honor
by translation into your tongue,
I honor your own to come,
I want my pen to be a part of them
(O you have a green, a green thumb).

2

The night of the duck dinner,
my third night in town,
you said (as they were dropping
brain onto my plate, and liver, and web):
"After this I must hurry home.
This is the night my epiphyllum blooms,
the one night in the year.
Last year my tree offered
eleven huge blooms,
huge white ones, lovely."
And *I* felt rushed, I hadn't
the rhythm of the place,
and you said:
"Man man lai — take your time."

3

Four of my poems you've done.
One about plants, about growing

(you have the greenest thumb),
two about birds —
and "Chickadee, Chickadee" becomes
"Hsiao niao, hsiao niao,
hsiao hua niao!"
The one about fall, where violins
drift into space, where birds
rise from iron, and gold
from out of our mouths,
you have had inked out
on a scroll, in characters,
and have given me.
You said: "It sounds revolutionary in Chinese."
And then: "I always love the word *space*,
it's good any time,
when I think of *space*,
I always feel nice."

4

You were hidden ten years.
Not that you took your time —
your time was taken from you.
You stayed inside the language,
never climbed, never showed yourself;
you slept.
I must tell you, my comrade poet,
how it is to see you open now —
forty poems, you say,
in the last year or so;
you've written me two already
since I've been here,
two poems to swell the forty,
huge ones, lovely.
I wish you always your stirring
out of the language, the freedom

to rise, to bloom as you please.
And *space*, Sister Epiphyllum,
space.

Zheng Min teaches at Beijing Normal University,
where I gave four weeks of lectures in September
1980. During the ten years of the "Cultural
Revolution" she did not write any poetry.

MARCH MORNING

Two little girls
coming down the sidewalk
dragging egg cartons on strings —
two clothespins stuck
on the front of each carton,
one at the back.
And when I ask them
what they are up to,
they yell:
> "The bugs are coming!
> The bugs are coming!"

NEIGHBOR IN MAY

my neighbor is hammering
and mending his house
he fixes in almost a frenzy
by night he dreams of his wife
dead nearly a year now
he dreams of nailing and healing
he dreams of repairing the damage

SEVEN SONGS FOR CHILDREN

DOCTOR LIVINGSTON

I took the dog for a walk in the park
There were snakes on the swings
There were goats in a tree
As we were rolling and running along
A camel came up and spoke to me:

Doctor Livingston, I presume
Diddledy Daddledy Doddledy Doo!

I went to the grocery store on the corner
Bought mustard and roses
Bought wine and baloney
As we were floating and fluttering home
I heard from the bag the Voice of Baloney:

Doctor Livingston, I presume
Diddledy Daddledy Doddledy Doo!

I love the rain
I love the snow
I love the street
I love my neighbors
My table is red
My ceiling is blue
My dog's vegetarian
How about you?

I wrote to my mother who lives underwater
I wrote to my brother
Who lives in a cloud
As we were wobbling and waddling back
The mailbox followed us, shouting out loud:

Doctor Livingston, I presume
Diddledy Daddledy Doddledy Doo!

I am the sun
I am the moon
I am a man
I'm marmalade too
My dog goes Miao
My cats go Moo
Doctor Livingston! Doctor Livingston!
Diddledy Daddledy Doddledy Doo!

TREE OF TWO BIRDS

Tree of two birds,
tree of two birds,
all winter long
I have heard your song,
and my heart has been like
a tree of two birds.

When it was cold, cold, cold,
when the snow flew,
when the clouds rode
down
        down
                down

such song
from the bare branch!
Sweet throat, sweet throat,
all winter long.

Even the darkest days
how you plant
your notes in my heart;
like a fountain,
green fountain in winter,
fountain of my friends,

like my family
singing to me,
O Brother,
O Sister
bird,
from the twigs of winter.

Tree of two birds,
tree of two birds,
feeding me with your song
all winter long.

STATE FAIR SONG

I want to learn to sleep
like the pigs at the State Fair;
oh, how those swine could sleep!

      Teach me! Teach me!

Like princes
in palaces
of straw

      Snore . . . Snore . . .

There they lay

      Snore . . . Snore . . .

Like hairy
like milky
kings
slumped on their thrones

      Snore . . . Snore . . .

There they lay

How do you do it, hogs?
The secret, the secret!
Snort me your secret
from the barns of sleep,
O swine!

      Teach me! Teach me!

    Snore . . .
        Snore . . .
           Snore . . .

SPRING SUITE

To Leaves, Late April

You timid leaves,
Now do your thing;
Let buds be bygones —
Be leaves, it's Spring!

Rain, Late April

Rain, O rain,
How green
You make this morning

And out in the woods
Are honest-to-goodness
Buds returning

And in you a robin
Atop a popple's
Piping and calling

A week of you
And all of my brain
Will be green

Green all my feeling
From your falling

It Must Be May

It must be May
When streams are swelling

It must be May
When birds are belling

It must be May
When buds are yelling

"Blossom or bust!"
(It must   it must)

May Slaps

I'm going to slap myself
Till I feel like a lilac

Slap!
     Slap!
          Slap!

There

REDWING BLACKBIRD

O
   O you
      O you red
         O you red wing
            O you red wing black
               O you red wing black bird
                  O you red wing black bird would
                     O you red wing black bird would be
                        O you red wing black bird would be a

SEVERE bird

but
   but for
      but for that
         but for that scar
            but for that scarlet

IMPROBABLE splash

on your sh
   on your shi
      on your ssssshhhhhhh iiiiinnnnn yyyyy

WINGS!

(this poem is best led by one voice, who feeds out the
phrases, which everyone else then repeats

body movements can be improvised on key words, especially
the final "shiny", which deserves something extravagant)

SOMETIMES THERE IS A LION

Sometimes there is a lion
a lion like this   (horizontal hand movement)

a lion like this   (vertical hand movement)

Sometimes there is a lion
in here   (point to heart)

Sometimes there is a roar
I hear   (hands over ears)

Sometimes there is sound
I am said to have made
but I did not, I did not   (hand over mouth)

Sometimes there is a cave
I go in   I come out
I go in   I come out   (point in and out to brain)

Sometimes there is a lion
by the sea
a water-liking lion   (paddling movement)

a lion *in* the sea   (swimming movement)

Sometimes there is a lion
up there   (point up)

a lion in air   (flying movement)

Sometimes a lion
escapes from me   (fast horizontal movements)

Don't shoot him!   (hands up)

CHILD'S ELM SONG

If there were no trees
I would take my turn
And stand in the street in spring
With arms wide open
In case there were birds
Who needed a place to sing.

THINKING I HEARD A CRY AMONG THE TREES

It could have been any creature
Could have been no cry

Something I thought I heard
As I ran that dirt road early

Could have been
In these miles and miles of forest
A tree itself

Some pine a wind has moaned around
Once too often
Some aspen too rotten

It could have been
A bird whose nest's taken
Or who takes another —
Its triumph

It could have been some creature
In a trap a man set
Or one by its own kind caught

It could have been
No cry

It could have been
Something not born for speech
The one time in time
It tries for its name
And fails

It could have been
The last of the dark's
Name for the last of the dark
Or the curse that the dark
In going
Calls to the first of the light

It could have been
Something I lack the means
To receive
Something I need to leave
The familiar for

Or it could have been
No cry
Nothing at all

No cry I heard
As I ran that early road

LEAVES ARE MY FLOWERS NOW

Leaves are my flowers now.
Basswood and sumac,
their banners and flags,
aspen and oak,
their shreds, their ribbons, their rags,
flutter and rattle.
Leaves are my flowers now.

Now is most fruit
shrunk to husk,
petal to small skull;
now are most things
gone from air,
now I see no dragonfly
out over water,
nor butterfly, with high sails
of yellow and black,
more beautiful than may be,
nor wasp, whom frosts
have silvered and slowed.
Now is light expert
among them, takes first
this pulse, then this one,
now shines a little
this surface, now
stains, now prescribes.

Clearer and clearer
the paths I pick.
Basswood and sumac,
their banners and flags,
aspen and oak,
their shreds, their ribbons, their rags,
flutter and rattle.
September is almost over
and leaves are my flowers now.

AT AVOCA

Meteors, August

Some spurt, some sputter,
some make a long easy arc
before they are done.
This loose fire among the fixed
we lie on our backs and wait for.
This able-to-fall,
this able-to-flame-and-be-gone.

To the Leaf, October

You are like something the sun
has fashioned from its own
flesh, and lets hang here. You
are scarcely solid. I could dream
you dissolve on my tongue.
I do not try
to touch you or take you.

The Bat that Got into the House

You will want to know what I did
after I found it stuck to the fly-paper
and fallen with it into the bath-tub,
after I watched it struggle and squeal,
the sickly glue-stuff half chewed through
and one wing waving. Reader, I drowned it.

One of my Trees has Caught the Moon

One of my trees has caught the moon.
As aspen, not a memorable one —

you know, a popple. That fat egg
is fairly snagged in its branches.
I don't care
if it's there in the morning or not —
one of my trees has caught the moon.
There's yellow all over its upper body.
I don't mind if it doesn't last long —
one of my trees has caught the moon.

SMOKE FROM THE FIRES

Smoke from the fires
Is in the rooms

However tight
You crank the windows

However you seal

Smoke from the fires
Is in the rooms

There must be ash
In the air

The hawk continues to fly
But becomes shabby
Scarlet a tanager
Ages before you

However close
You pull in your horns

However you smile
However you turn away

For all your building
For all your skills

Smoke from the fires
Is in the rooms

POEM

I dreamed I was a bird.
Not that there was flight.
Instead I stood
on my claws and pecked
at some black meat on the ground.
You'd have to turn off the highway
and down dirt roads to find me.
Not that I recommend it.
Not that I was of the kind who sings.
Not that the bird had wings.

CUTTING UP A FALLEN TREE

When I cut up wood, I like to wear loose old
clothes — check shirt, overalls, some kind of country
cap. That way my body feels free behind the cold
historical arm.

And I aim the twentieth century at the tree. I make
any amount of cold children. These oak boys and girls
I carry in armfuls into the house, I bed them snug in
the bin. My boots are heavy, like a soldier's.

When I take the chain-saw to this wood, it seems that
I am cutting up an old old woman, a dried one, all sap
gone. I'm taking this crone apart. And I feel the
presence of the hag in me. She wants to wither something
in my life. An old old girl would dance with me. A witch
would be my bride.

Oak the sacred. Oak royal. Oak of cults. "Door"
in many tongues. Oak hard. Best burner. "The fuel of
the midsummer fire is always oak."

With the brain timber I dream. I am walking a
rough road; cold scald of moonlight. I sense a daughter,
and a son. And there my wife Birch, she I do not touch
nor feed to my fire. Whose head in a white breeze
dances. How graceful my wife. How lovely is Thy light,
O Lord, about her leaves.

ALL MY PRETTY ONES

a cycle of eight poems
for music by Stephen Paulus

in memory of Anne Sexton

"Everything in me is a bird"

(the singer is a woman)

1/ IN A TREE AT DAWN, TO LISTEN TO BIRDS

I had wanted to hide.
I had wanted to stay there and hear
the whole day's songs.

I who am not satisfied
with my speech,
so heavy, so human,
I had wanted to learn their lightness,

I who am not pleased
with my name,
I had hoped they would think me
their fellow among the green
and fling me a new one.

When I had climbed back down
to where I belong,
among women, among men,
the singing began again.

2/ AND THE BIRDS ARRIVE

And the birds arrive.
It means it is morning,
it means it is day.
The night tree shakes them out.

This is a life lived alone.
This is a life lived like a tree.
This tree waits for its birds.

I don't remember the dream.
I keep the image of a courtyard.

I have lost my people of the dream.

Now my dawn company has come.
The guests, for feeding.
It means it is morning,
it means it is day.

Still I want the dream. The Delicate.
There I fly to feed.
I have lost my people of the dream.

And the birds arrive.
As sons, as daughters, they will do.
They sing the light into change.
Among sunflower, cracked corn.
For light alone they sing,
the feeders sway.

It means it is morning,
it means it is day.

3/ PURPLE FINCH

A finch with a broken neck lies by my house.
I must assume the coroner of birds would say
the neck was broken.
I suppose he flew against my window.
I take the sharp spade and dig
through the first snow. The ground
is not yet frozen, but hardening.
I dig through a thick root.
I dig past where the dogs would reach,
who are watching.
I dig through the old worlds,

where the worms still rule.
I dig past the gates and exits of that.
I dig through five kinds of color.
I dig through gold and blue and scarlet and black and green.
I dig past color.
I dig till I feel I have reached
air again,
air of a quieter kind,
where he can ride,
in a time of waiting.
With a mind for all who descend
I lower the broken bird.

4/ FEEDER

The same day I build
a feeder for the winter birds,
two grosbeaks, male and female,
are feeding there.
His chest is yellow, bright,
hers milder, a kind of gray.
The feeder is fixed to a bare tree,
whose leaves these birds become,
female and male leaves,
both bright and mild.

5/ LITTLE LIFE

Life,
O little life,
what is happening to you?

You one among many,
don't you like to be
just a tree of the wood?

O little life,
let the birds come down
on you,

let them sing
above your speech,
which should diminish,

let the rains wet
you, let storms shake
you — and shine with your storm.

The earth lies deep
where your roots grip —
and your arms in air —

she guards the seeds
of space in her;
you are feeding there.

Life,
O little life,
it is happening to you.

6/ THE BIRD INSIDE

And when I am calm
the bird arrives inside.
Who slows between the eyes.
Who spreads long wings.

This is he and she of the center.
Wing Shadow. Wing Light.
And stands. And stands.
Without memory. Without desire.

Who comes when I am calm.

Who stands at the center.
Who does not feed, nor sing.
Without memory. Without desire.

Who grows. Till the skull fill,
till all my head be bird,
bird-bones be mine, and I rise.
Without memory. Without desire.

7/ NIGHT BIRD

I know what the night bird wants

choose   choose   choose   choose
        easy   easy   easy   easy

just under tongues
the night bird lives

night bird among the leaves

she has wings enough
for everyone
there is milk enough
in that breast for feeding

choose   choose   choose   choose
        easy   easy   easy   easy

she has a new name in mind
each to receive the new name
hidden just under
hidden just under
the old one

who out there, but near . . .
who nearer . . .
who nearer . . .

now   now   now   now
    in   in   in   in

O Mother of Bones
Mother of Names

I know what the night bird wants

8/ ALL MY PRETTY ONES

Do you see? There!
It is the grosbeak   it is the chickadee
come to crack
seeds, seeds I have set out
it is the purple finch   it is the gold

All my pretty
        all my pretty
                all my pretty ones
return

Do you hear? There!
thrum!   thrum!
wind of their wings
some singly   some paired
some with their tribe
some with a quick, a silvery
some with a slower singing

All my pretty

        all my pretty

                all my pretty ones

return

I had forgotten
I had feared to wake to songs
which ask that all of the heart be used

How many dyings
and still this singing
no question of no song
from the breast intended for singing

I had wanted to hide . . .

Do you see? There!
at dawn now
        from darkness
                from dream

Do you hear? There!
in light now
        from shelter
                from sleep

it is the nuthatch   it is the sparrow
the thrush   the cardinal   the jay

O little life

All my pretty

        all my pretty

                all my pretty ones

return

4

HIDING FROM THE BRIDE

I was to hide in the long grass
And you to find me

But first to wash my face
In the slow water of the river —
Really several strands of stream

Bending my hand down and to
Smear a little night water
Over cheeks and eyes and brow

And to lie down in the long grass then
And you to find me

And you in a far corner of the meadow
Quietly counting   preparing

And I choosing my place
And lying down close to the ground
And not to care what night creatures
Might crawl over me

And you with your lamp to come
Like a warm wind
Setting the meadow in motion

To where I lay in the long ground
Panting

And to dig me up again

ARROGANCE

1

River, so fast, so swollen,
like a field in flood,
like wide ploughland sliding,
with ice, with foam
on your scrambling surface —
I fear the dogs
gulping at the edge
will be swept away by you.
I could be taken too.

2

I was leaving, angry.
I would not meet my wife's eye.
I felt poison as
I laced up my boots.
I thought then,
what have I to lose by going
back up the stair?
What I have to lose is
my arrogance, that sense
of separateness I feed.
I went back
up the stair, boots laced,
and bent over the bed;

and began to hold her.
Thoughts rolled from me
in a sweat,
and I murmured things to my wife.

3

I want to be like you, river.
Help me to break
my arrogance, please.
I want to crumble, loosen, slide,
all my sweaty surface littered
with the bits of arrogance
being born away.
Let the dogs or her or anyone
take pleasure at the sight
of my arrogance bits going by.

LOVE POEM, EASTER SATURDAY

In a hunger not like any other
All the things of the deep
Rise   rise
And shaking their flesh from the surface
Take to the sky

While all things of the air
From heights little and great
Dive   dive
In a flood in a thunder of feathers
And are one with the waters

HER GARDEN

Nothing will save the leaves.
And all blossom be gone.
And since you must be in the city,
I am seeing it for you, one last time,
before a frost finds it.
And tonight I keep the yard light on,
way past dusk, into night;
I am keeping the watch for you
on this vigil of frost.

The broad squash leaves remind me
of lotus, the sea-green
fans I saw in China;
and when I put my nose
in among the tomatoes,
I have to keep on going
down, down, to where
the shiny ones lie, sunken.
Here too zucchini, gleaming in secret.

The leathery lanterns of pepper,
the satin clubs of egg-plant
that lengthen along the ground,
the squash, globed in its green armor,
its leaves outrunning their fence,
tentacling toward the woodpile,
the carrots, embedded,
and potatoes, more mildly hidden —
such loot, booty, plunder for hands.
And I will bring them.

As for the flowers, their story is all in air.
The zinnia, scarlet, like some shaggy

pine-cone, brushes my shoulder.
Paler the splintry sprays of cosmos.
Below them, blue
tufts and clusters of bachelor buttons ·
from seeds we were given in England
five years ago.
And up the west wall the morning glories.

In a year I was not fair to you,
you gave me two apple-trees;
when things were worse,
you planted winter bulbs.
One bleak April morning
two crocus surprised me —
no, two crocus *amazed* —
spearing up through dead leaves.

This night, at the seasons's turn —
the season of dreaming, you say —
when the brain is lit and flickering
with immense aurora,
before a frost grips, crumpling,
before its wires drag down
all you have sown,
here, with a now quiet heart, beside
what continues to breathe, reach, open —
insisting on living —
I am keeping the watch for you.

> *for Lisa*
> *also for John Gardner*

9/15/82

TO MY WIFE IN TIME OF WAR

1/ Drawing of a Woman's Torso (Leonardo da Vinci)

First, taking one of the branch
lines in the system of tubes around
the central system you come
at the end of the line to a small
town, a village really. Here
you may wander for hours, in dust,
dried mud. Find no one. Just
here a pair of boots, here a
table, set for a meal, no one,
here a ladder to be raised
but ladder on its side, no
climber and no hold in the sky,
no rungs for the climbing. To
get back, you cannot. What is there
for you, anyway, in the central
system.

Below the innominate vein, the no
name. Down this way
the liver, but the liver
is sleeping. Across
from the liver the spleen but
the spleen is sleeping. Kidney
also. But this is not
for hibernation, show no one
their room. No "little blankets,"
stuffed toys, no outsize bright
posters, show no one
their room, ash that has entered
their room, ash and no song, no
ladder and no
climber and no hold in the sky,
no rungs for the climbing.

Lower, the main vein. Here
where even no small
towns. Not one
dog. Nicht. Niente. Nothing. No
thing. Dust ruts scars.

Forest on each side, thick. Hundreds
of miles of this. No
stopping. When you are out of
fuel, keep going. No running
water, rest area, comfort
station, car wash, not one
town, no one, no rungs
for the climbing.

Pelvis now. Things
have been carved here, scrawled
scratched smeared carved
on the walls, were there light
you could make them
out but there is none. Dark.
Sailors going down wrote
here, their boats wrote on
the walls. The car wreck, three
teenagers, wrote. The rape
wrote here. On these walls
the whales wrote. The buffalo.
And we were here. Dust.
Ladder to be raised but ladder
on its side, no
climber and no hold
in the sky, no rungs
for the climbing.

2/ Tap

I know, Anton Chekhov, why you say: "There ought to be,
behind the door of every happy contented man, someone standing

with a hammer reminding him with a tap that there are unhappy people."

Have happy. Have hammer. Am my hammer.
Tap.

Ach, Bertolt Brecht, such a hard time you gave Andre Gide for writing in his wartime journal in praise of a giant plane tree — its enormous trunk, mighty branching and its equilibrium. In California you disapproved, shaking your head. You say that talk about trees is close to a crime. In the dark times, only the dark singing.

Tap.

She, pregnant ten weeks, has dreamed of a tree at the family home, which reaches now far past its real height, to the ledge of the third floor room which was hers. All springs of her girlhood, it would hold at least one nest, and now several, each with its young birds, which their mothers are feeding. These birds are yellow and black, the color of grosbeaks, and the topmost ones have tiny ears, like mice ears. And Lisa chooses to water the birds with a watering can, the way you sprinkle a spring garden, she says, its buds, to keep it growing. And says: "I was delighted with this dream."

I have been teaching the time's poems. When Avrom my student asks if all poets must go through such darkness, I tell of Roethke walking into the room of students, his "Help me." Once, when I ask Avrom how he is feeling, he says: "Afraid."

Tap.

3/ Living Body

But there is one I know of now
beneath a tree, floating

76

in placenta shade, furled
Buddha of seventy days within
the body of the living woman.
Who still weighs
              "less than an aspirin."
Rudimentary, a heart is beating.

I don't know what song's to be made.
I can't have the geese, now
in their season of returning, fashion
it for me. Nor you robins, with your
ripe clear calling. But never
to be dictated into no song.
                        Wife,
do I warble there are robins
                   in your body?
Can they accuse me of wafting
                   geese through your limbs?

I say, there is a traveler toward you.
I say, the tree is occupied.
I say, some kind of song.

 Last I call you to witness,
Teilhard de Chardin, who said:
"The earth is building. . . the earth
is an immense groping."
                   Who are *you*,
ten weeks of cells blind inside my love,
but a groping? How to serve you
the news of the qualifying of song?
Only the tapping? Only
the darker singing?
                   Shatter
the robins, then, bring down

the geese with hammers.
Cancel all greening. Revoke returning.
The earth is an immense groping.
How long?
        How long?

I don't know what it can be,
what I can have for you,
                little one,
though it will be waiting.
I don't know
        what kind of song.

1982

The Granary, Kim R. Stafford

Calling the Dead, C. G. Hanzlicek

Dreams Before Sleep, T. Alan Broughton

Sorting it Out, Anne S. Perlman

Love Is Not a Consolation; It Is a Light, Primus St.
John

1983

The Going Under of the Evening Land, Mekeel
McBride

Museum, Rita Dove

Air and Salt, Eve Shelnutt

Nightseasons, Peter Cooley

1984

Falling From Stardom, Jonathan Holden

Miracle Mile, Ed Ochester

Girlfriends and Wives, Robert Wallace

Earthly Purposes, Jay Meek

Not Dancing, Stephen Dunn

The Man in the Middle, Gregory Djanikian

A Heart Out of This World, David James

All You Have in Common, Dara Wier

1985

Smoke From the Fires, Michael Dennis Browne

Full of Lust and Good Usage, Stephen Dunn (2nd.
edition)

Far and Away, Mark Jarman